A Young Christian Book for Girls

Everybody Needs a Friend

Barbara DeGrote-Sorensen

D1525036

AUGSBURG Publishing House • Minneapolis

EVERYBODY NEEDS A FRIEND
A Young Christian Book for Girls

Scripture quotations unless otherwise noted are from Today's English Version of the Bible, copyright 1976, American Bible Society, and are used by permission.

Photos: Dave Anderson, 12; Gail B. Int Veldt, 24; Jean-Claude Lejeune, 38, 78, 88; Jim Whitmer, 50; L. S. Stepanowiez, Panographics, 60; Mary Harrison, 96.

Library of Congress Cataloging-in-Publication Data

DeGrote-Sorensen, Barbara, 1954–
  EVERYBODY NEEDS A FRIEND.

  Summary: Brief stories and devotions examine the responsibilities, problems, and pleasures of friendship.
  1. Friendship—Religious aspects—Christianity—
Juvenile literature.   2. Girls—Religious life.
[1. Friendship.   2. Prayer books and devotions.
3. Christian life]   I. Title.
BV4647.F7S67   1987   248.8'2   86-32152
ISBN 0-8066-2247-4

Manufactured in the U.S.A.   APH 10-2120

1   2   3   4   5   6   7   8   9   0   1   2   3   4   5   6   7   8   9

To David, my forever friend

Contents

About This Book

Dear Young Christian,

It's not always easy being a friend. Choosing friends and keeping them is a tricky business. Think about the friends you have right now. Why do you like them? How did you get to be friends? What things do you both like to do? How do you feel about yourself when you are with your friends? How do your parents feel about your friends?

Who you choose as friends says something about you. Do you really like your friends, or do you just like to be part of their crowd? Can you share your friends with other people, or do you like to keep them all to yourself? When your friends disappoint you, how do you handle it? Do you change friends as often as you change clothes? What does it mean to be a friend—to have a friend?

9

Questions! Questions! Questions! Friends can be fun. But sometimes friendships are a lot of hard work. You know what it feels like when your best friend is mad at you. Pit in the stomach. Hard to concentrate on school work. You may not even feel like going to school. Sometimes it may seem like friends just aren't worth the trouble. But deep down you need your friends and they need you. That's what friends are for—to be there for each other.

The girls you will meet in this book are a lot like you. Jena, Stacey, Kim, Beth, Kayla, Megan, and Renee all have learned something special about being a friend. Let them become your friends as you share their thoughts and adventures. And while you are at it, don't forget that Jesus, the one who is always there for you, will be reading right along with you.

Jesus is the ultimate friend. He knows how important friends are to you. He had friends himself. He knows all about the business of friendship. Just ask him.

You can read this book by yourself or share it with your friends and family. At the beginning of each chapter you will find a Bible verse chosen to help lead you into the story. A closing prayer and action idea will follow.

Read! Enjoy! Make Friends! And begin to find out—just what friends are for.

A friend in Christ,
Barbara DeGrote-Sorensen

"I have also learned why people work so hard
to succeed: it is because they envy the things
their neighbors have. But it is useless.
It is like chasing the wind."
—Ecclesiastes 4:4

•

*"Why does Karen always get everything she wants?
Just once I'd like to come in first!" Jena cried.*

Chasing the Wind

1

"Students of St. John Middle School—your next student body president—*Karen O'Halloran!* Let's give her a round of applause," announced Principal Butler.

The students erupted into wild cheers. "KA-REN! KA-REN! KA-REN!" they chanted over and over, pounding their feet on the floor until the room rumbled and the lights shook in the ceiling.

Jena Cole stood in the back under one of the exit signs, watching the crowd and the smiling Karen. She wasn't surprised at the outcome of the campaign. Jena had said it many times—"Whatever Karen wants, Karen gets!" But Jena had wanted something too—a little recognition, her name on a poster, or maybe even a few chants of "Je-na! Je-na!" would have been nice. But campaign managers don't get the glory. They just put up the posters and take them

11

down. "Might as well start now," Jena said half aloud as she begin pulling at a "Karen for President" poster above the door.

"Hey Jena! Why aren't you in there with the rest of those wild and crazy people," Joe laughed from the hallway.

Jena turned and smiled. If Joe were a girl he would have been her best friend. As it was, he was just a pal. "A campaign manager's job is never done," said Jena, forcing a laugh. "But Karen won and that's what matters, I guess."

"Well, if it were up to me you would be up on that stage right now," Joe said. "Why didn't you run for president?"

"Me!" Jena laughed for real. "Run against Karen? You've got to be kidding!"

"Why not? You've got everything Karen's got. You're popular. You're smart and you get things done. People like you," Joe said matter-of-factly.

"Well, maybe next year," Jena said, picking up a piece of poster that had fallen.

Joe pushed the outside door open. "My mom's picking me up for a dentist appointment. Gotta go. Think about it!" he said over his shoulder.

Run against Karen. Jena managed a weak smile. *Joe can be so out of it sometimes.*

And yet Jena couldn't forget his words—*You've got everything Karen's got. People like you. People like you.*

Jena turned back to the noisy gymnasium. Karen was still standing by the microphone as she smiled and waved to the crowd. "KA-REN! KA-REN!" the crowd continued its chanting. Deep in Jena's heart a little voice chanted back—"JE-NA! JE-NA! JE-NA!"

Jena's prayer: Dear Jesus, is it wrong to want to come out first once in a while? Your disciples used to argue about who would be first. I remember what you told them. But, Jesus—it seems like I never win! Amen.

2

"Tell Karen congratulations!" a girl yelled from across the hallway.

"Bet you're really proud of Karen!" Mrs. Turner, the Home Ec teacher had said during first hour.

Karen, Karen, Karen. All I hear is, Karen! Jena mused to herself as she raced up the steps toward her English classroom. She just wanted to get to class before anyone had any more "Karen comments" to make.

Jena bounded up the second flight of steps. A large group of girls was chatting away at the top of the steps. Karen, as usual, was in the middle of them all. Jena kept her eyes down and tried to hurry past without being noticed.

"Jena!" Karen yelled, excusing herself from the group. "Where were you yesterday after the rally? We looked all over for you. A bunch of us went downtown for pizza to celebrate. We missed you."

"Sorry," Jena paused, "I just—had a few things to do. Mr. Butler wanted all the campaign posters down right away and—well, I'm really glad you won, Karen," Jena said, trying to sound sincere.

Karen laughed. "That's Jena! All work and no play. Listen—I know how hard you worked on the campaign. Harder than anyone, including me. Thanks for being such a great friend. I won't forget it!"

Jena smiled sadly. *A great friend? It's a good thing Karen can't read my mind,* Jena thought as she opened the door to Mr. Lantz's room. *Karen said it herself,* Jena's thoughts continued. *I worked harder than anyone. It isn't fair that Karen gets all the attention and I get—to be proud of her.*

Jena plunked her books down on her desk and looked around the room. Joe waved from the back corner where Mr. Lantz had set up a reading center. It was neat. A couple of bean bag chairs and a few posters. Kids who finished their work early got to go back there as a reward.

Jena like English mainly because she liked Mr. Lantz. She liked the way he made a person feel as if you could do anything. He was always saying, "Go for it! Go for it!" He said it so much that kids called him "Gopher" outside of class. He didn't seem to mind.

"Find your seats please, ladies and gentlemen," Mr. Lantz called out as he finished taping a large red and yellow poster to the right-hand corner of the chalkboard.

Joe tapped Jena on the shoulder. "Do you have an extra pencil I could borrow?" he whispered. "I've already forgotten mine twice." Jena nodded and handed him a new one. Pencils were very important to Mr. Lantz. So were assignments and paying attention in class. The penalty for forgetting a pencil, an assignment, or "your head," as Mr. Lantz put it, was a one-minute impromptu speech on a topic like shoelaces or fingernails. Mr. Lantz always managed to think of something. Joe's last speech had been on toasters. It was embarrassing.

16

"Before we begin today's assignment," Mr. Lantz said, sitting on the edge of his desk, "I have an announcement about a special opportunity that I hope will interest many of you." He pointed to the poster he had just taped to the board. "The St. John's Community Theatre is planning to perform the musical *Annie*. It requires a number of roles for young people, including the lead role of Annie."

Jena loved the theatre. She had taken dance since she could walk, and everyone said she had a strong voice. She'd already had a few walk-on parts in some of the plays her mother had been in.

Jena quietly hummed one of the tunes from the musical as she envisioned herself on stage, the crowd applauding as she took her solo bow.

"JE-NA! JE-NA! JE-NA!" they roared together as she bowed again and again.

"Jena! Jena! Earth to Jena!" Mr. Lantz said with a laugh.

Jena's head snapped and she looked up to see Mr. Lantz standing next to her desk. The other kids chuckled as he dished out the penalty—a one-minute speech on daydreaming!

Jena's prayer: Lord, I'm so excited and nervous about the tryouts for Annie. *I just have to get the lead, Lord. I just* have *to! Amen.*

3

"But mother!" Jena cried. "I could do it. Really!"

"I don't know, Jena," Mrs. Cole said, putting down her coffee cup. "It would mean weeks of night rehearsals. Saturdays, too. You've been so busy lately with the campaign. Why don't you just take it easy for a while, honey? You don't have to be involved in everything."

"But I want to," Jena complained. "It could be my big chance to be a star!"

"A lot of girls will want the lead, Jena," her mother warned. "And being the star isn't always fun. It's a lot of responsibility, too."

Jena looked gloomily at the two peanut butter cookies on her plate. "Don't you think I have a chance?" she asked quietly.

Mrs. Cole pulled a stool up to the kitchen counter. "No, you have a good chance. Probably one of the best. But what's important is that you enjoy whatever part you get, even if that means enjoying it from the audience. You don't have to be a star to be a winner, you know," she said as she pushed a lock of hair behind Jena's ear.

"Oh, mother," Jena whined, "you don't understand. Just look at the campaign. Karen always gets what she wants. Just once I'd like to come in first!"

"Now, listen here," Mrs. Cole said as she took Jena's hands. "You're not great because of what others think of you. You're great because of what God thinks of you. God made you and God thinks you're terrific. So do your dad and I!"

"OK! OK!" Jena said with a little laugh. "But you're my parents. You have to like me!" Jena gulped the rest of her milk. "So can I try out for the play?" she asked again.

"If you really want to—yes," Mrs. Cole said smiling. "But Annie or no Annie, remember that you've already won."

The phone on the kitchen counter rang twice.

"I'll get it!" Jena said, jumping off the stool. "It's probably Joe, wanting to know tomorrow's assignment."

Jena picked up the phone. "Hi—this is Jena."

"Hi, Jena. Karen here. Just calling to see if I can catch a ride with you to the tryouts on Friday. My mom has a late appointment and can't pick me up. You're going, aren't you?" Karen asked.

Jena felt as if someone had punched her in the stomach. "Ah—I guess so," Jena stumbled. "We're leaving from the east parking lot after school. At least that's where we usually meet."

"Great!" said Karen. "See you there, and break a leg!"

Jena hung the phone up and sighed. "Karen O'-Halloran," she whispered, "this time it's my turn."

Jena's prayer: I know you love me, Lord, and I'm sorry I feel so angry toward Karen. It's not really her fault. She can't help if she wins all the time. Help me just to do my best on Friday and be happy with the results. Amen.

4

"Next, please!" the middle-aged woman wearing a black leotard called from the judges' table.

Jena took two deep breaths as she climbed up the steps to the stage microphone. She was surprised how nervous she felt as she looked out over the faces of the others waiting their turn to audition. There were more kids trying out than anyone had expected. Some had even come from other towns nearby.

Jena's dancing audition had gone well. She knew all the steps from dance class and just had to put them in the right order with the music. It had been a snap. When she had finished, the judges had whispered excitedly and given an enthusiastic nod.

"Tell us when you're ready, dear," the woman in black said with a warm smile.

Jena caught her mom's and dad's eyes and smiled as they waved and gave her a thumbs-up sign. The piano player began the introduction as Jena stepped to the microphone and began to sing. Her clear voice carried across the gym and echoed off the back wall.

When she finished, the crowd applauded approvingly. Jena's heart was beating a mile a minute. She had done her best. Now she had to wait with the others.

"Great job, Jena!" Karen whispered as Jena sank back into her chair.

Jena turned around and gave Karen a quick smile. "Thanks! Sorry I missed yours. I forgot my dance shoes in the car and had to go get them. How did you do?" Jena asked, not really wanting to know.

Karen looked concerned. "I don't know. I think I did OK. But you never know with these things. Sometimes you win. Sometimes you don't."

"You've got to be kidding!" Jena exclaimed. "You always win. In fact, I almost didn't come when I knew you were going to try out!"

"Whatever Karen wants, Karen gets?" said Karen with a knowing look in her eye.

Jena squirmed. "Guess someone's been blabbing at school. Look—I'm sorry you heard that. I guess I was kind of jealous of all the attention you were getting after you won the campaign. But we—you do always seem to come out first in everything." Jena stopped short. She hadn't meant to say all that. Especially to Karen.

The two girls looked at each other in silence.

"Look, Jena—I have won sometimes, but there are a lot of things I've wanted that I couldn't have." Karen's eyes filled with tears. "Like a mom who isn't always too busy. Or parents who live together." Karen paused. "You've already come in first and you don't even know it!"

Jena didn't know what to say.

"Here come the judges," Karen whispered. "Good luck!"

"You too, Karen," Jena said. "I really mean it!"

The woman in the black leotard waited by the microphone for everyone's attention. "Well, it was a hard decision," she announced. "We will start with the walk-on parts and save the role of Annie for last." The crowd murmured excitedly. "OK, please come forward as your name is called."

One by one Karen and Jena watched as those around them squealed with delight and ran up on the stage as their names were called.

"Karen O'Halloran!" the woman said in a loud voice to be heard over the growing commotion on stage.

Karen squeezed Jena's hand. "I'll see you up there," she whispered, and then ran to join the others on stage.

Jena's heart pounded faster than before. There were only two roles left. One for a boy and one for the part of Annie.

"Scott Smith!" the woman yelled out. A small boy with curly black hair jumped out of this seat with a yelp and the crowd laughed.

"And now, before we announce the final choice for our leading lady, the judges would like to thank all of you for auditioning today. You are all winners because you believed in yourselves enough to try out. We liked what we saw today. Please try again next year." The woman paused dramatically as she looked over the list of names. "For the role of Annie, please congratulate—Jena Cole!"

Before she knew it, Jena was surrounded by swarms of people, all calling out her name.

"We're proud of you, honey," her mom whispered in her ear as her dad gave her a peck on the cheek.

Karen was waiting off on the side. "You won, Jena!" she beamed.

"In more ways than one," Jena said as she ran to hug her friend. "In more ways than one!"

Jena's prayer: Lord, thank you for all the times I have won and didn't even know it! Help me to see and understand all you have already done for me. By the way, Lord, I think you're terrific, too. Amen.

Action idea: Write a letter to a friend or someone close, saying you're proud of the person. Tell your friend what you like about him or her. Make the person feel like a winner.

"A friend means well, even when he hurts you.
But when an enemy puts his arm around
your shoulders—watch out!"
—Proverbs 27:6

•

*"She's worse than a liar. She's a fake!" Stacey
shouted. "She only pretended to be my friend."*

Faker

1

Stacey Simons pulled on her favorite purple tur-
tleneck and gave her hair its daily two tugs. It seemed
as if she'd been growing her hair out forever. Right
now it was in that awful, in-between stage—too short
to pull back and too long to leave hanging in your
eyes.

"Maybe I should have it feathered in front like
Jennifer Owens. Her hair always looks perfect," Stacey sighed as she hunted in her closet for her button-
fly jeans.

*Of course Jennifer Owens is perfect—the most pop-
ular girl in the entire eighth grade class—she even beat
out Melanie Peterson for first chair in band*, Stacey
thought. *Last spring Jennifer got her picture in the paper
for winning the girl's individual track event, too.*

Even her teeth are perfect. Stacey ran her tongue
over the clear plastic retainer she was supposed to
wear faithfully for the next two years.

"Some people just have it all!" she muttered, picking up her books and pack from where she had dumped them the night before.

"Hurry it up, Stacey! Dad's waiting," her brother Steve hollered from the downstairs entry.

"Coming!" Stacey shouted back, shoving the rest of her things into the already stuffed backpack.

Stacey and her brother always got a ride to school with their dad. Since the junior high and senior high had joined the year before, he could drop them both off and still make it to the office by 8:15.

"It's about time, Chubbs," Steve said to Stacey, tousling her carefully combed hair. "I've got to talk to Coach Robbins before the first bell."

Stacey hated it when Steve called her "Chubbs." It had been cute when she was little, but who wanted to be in eighth grade and still be called "Chubbs"?

"Knock it off, Steve! And quit calling me Chubbs! You're always treating me like your baby sister!" Stacey yelled as she frantically combed her hair.

"You *are* my baby sister," Steve teased.

"Dad!" Stacey turned to Mr. Simons for support. "Do something!"

"Let's move it, guys!" Mr. Simons said, ignoring the squabble. "We're going to have to make all the green lights today!"

Stacey checked the new digital watch she had gotten last Christmas from her parents—7:55—plenty of time.

"I've got a few phone calls to make," Mr. Simons continued. "Someone had the phone tied up last night," he said, giving Steve a good-natured nudge.

"Just a few members of my ever-growing fan club," Steve joked, checking his teeth in the mirror on the right visor.

"An all-girl fan club," Stacey pointed out with a hint of disgust in her voice. "I'll never call a boy at home. I'd rather die first." She continued making a face to prove her point.

"I'm not complaining," Steve said from the front seat. "When you've got it—you've got it! What's a guy supposed to do?"

"Oh, put a lid on it, Steve!" Stacey said dryly. "You're not as perfect as you think!"

"Just ask my fan club," Steve said with a wink as Mr. Simons stopped to let him off. "They don't seem to mind my few imperfections."

"Never mind, Steve," Mr. Simons said. "See you tonight, and try to keep your mind on your game, OK?"

Stacey's prayer: *Lord, I know I can't be perfect, but it's hard not to compare myself to others. Sometimes I feel so ugly and awful. How could anyone like me? Yes, I know that you love me. But you like everybody. Well, at least that's one. Thanks, Lord. Amen.*

2

Stacey scanned the crowded hallway of South Junior High for her best friend Julie.

"Wonder where she could be?" Stacey thought aloud as she shifted her books from one arm to the other.

"Stacey!" an overly friendly voice called from a large group of girls across the hall.

Stacey turned, expecting to see Julie's bright red hair and big glasses. Instead, the perfectly straight teeth of Jennifer Owens smiled back at her.

Something that felt like a large cottonball settled somewhere between Stacey's tonsils and stomach. She tried to act normal, but she could feel the red creeping into her face. She always turned red when she was nervous. It was a dead giveaway.

Jennifer didn't seem to notice. "Stacey Simons? Steve Simon's sister?" Jennifer asked, shuffling through her assortment of books, folders, and loose papers.

Stacey chewed on her lip and wished Julie would hurry up and get there.

Jennifer continued looking through her stuff, finally pulling a small, pink envelope from between two library books.

"I'm having a party at my house after the game on Friday. You're invited," she said brusquely as she handed Stacey the pink invitation.

Stacey looked at the envelope with "Stacey Simons" printed across the front in large letters. The group of girls from across the hall had stopped talking and were watching intently.

"Uh—I don't know, I've got to talk to—" Stacey stammered.

Jennifer scowled. She wasn't used to getting less than an overly excited reply. "Look. We're just going to have pizza and watch a video. You can bring a friend if you want," Jennifer said in an impatient voice.

Stacey took the pink envelope and stuck it into her math notebook. "I'll have to check with my folks first. I'll let you know tomorrow," she managed to say.

Jennifer looked relieved. "Great!" she said as the friendliness returned to her voice. Jennifer motioned for the group of girls to join her.

"But I—" Stacey began.

"Hey girls! Stacey can come," Jennifer yelled to the others.

"Is she bringing Steve?" a loud-voiced girl shouted. The others laughed so hard that other students looked to see what was going on.

Stacey managed a slight smile, trying to feel like she was part of the conversation.

Jennifer ignored the other girl's comment. "See you on Friday then, Stacey?" Jennifer asked, smiling her most charming smile. Not waiting for an answer she turned and headed towards homeroom.

"See ya, Stacey!"

"Yeah—bye, Stacey!"

"Catch you later, Stacey!"

Stacey leaned back against a row of lockers. *I'm in! I can't believe it! Jennifer Owens invited me to her party. I didn't even know she knew my name!*

Stacey smiled, tugged on her hair two times, and joined the few students still trying to make it to class before the final bell.

I'm in! she repeated to herself as she opened the door to Mr. Olson's room.

She liked the thought.

Stacey's prayer: *I don't know how you did it, Lord. It's a miracle. I should be feeling great, but something doesn't seem quite right. Now that I'm "in" I'm not sure I really want to be. I don't mean to seem ungrateful, but I'm not sure I really like Jennifer Owens and her friends. Oh well, what's important is that they like me, right, Lord? Amen.*

3

"You're kidding!" Julie screamed over the phone. "Jennifer Owens' party? Are you sure she said I could come?" she questioned for the third time.

"She said I could bring a friend," Stacey repeated. "You've got to come. I'd die if I had to go alone!"

"We were going to my aunt's house this weekend, but maybe I could talk them into leaving me home. Those trips are so boring." Julie groaned, remembering the last visit to Aunt Connie's.

"You could sleep over," Stacey suggested. "Steve could pick us up at school, and you could stay at our house. We'll have a lot to talk about."

Julie jumped at the opportunity. "Super! But I'll have to check it out with my folks first."

Stacey paused and sighed. "Got to go, Julie. Steve wants to phone—again."

Three days later Stacey and Julie climbed the steps leading to the front porch of Jennifer's house. Jennifer answered the bell on the second ring.

"Hi. We're all downstairs," she said, leading the two girls through the kitchen and down the basement steps. "Stacey's here," she yelled loudly over the music.

"That sure doesn't look like Steve," the loud-mouthed girl from the day before said, pointing at Julie. The other girls snickered.

"This is Julie," Stacey said to the group, but no one seemed to care.

"Steve sure did a great job at the game tonight!" Jennifer purred. "Didn't he, girls?" Eight heads bobbed up and down in agreement. "I don't suppose he's at home yet?" Jennifer directed her question at Stacey.

"Probably," Stacey said, popping potato chips into her mouth. "He's got to work tomorrow, early."

"I'm going to watch TV," Julie announced, heading for the family room sofa.

"Well—" Jennifer paused, looking at the others. "We were just talking about how much fun it would be to call Steve Simons and tell him what a super job he did. Sixteen points and twelve rebounds!"

"You want to call my brother?" Stacey said as she stopped chewing.

"We thought you might call him for us." Jennifer pushed. "Tell him a few of your friends just want to say hi." Jennifer paused and waited. So did the other girls in the room.

"This is a joke, right?" Stacey laughed. "Steve would kill me!" Stacey looked around. No one else was laughing.

"Come on, Stacey. Call him," Jennifer said again.

"Yeah, Stacey. Do it!" the others chimed in.

Stacey looked at the white wall phone hanging next to the door. Someone had tied a hangman's noose with the cord. Stacey didn't think that was too funny, considering the situation she was presently in.

Stacey picked up the phone and dialed her number. Steve answered in a sleepy voice.

"Steve? This is Stacey. No, not Stacey Lehman. Stacey your sister. Some of the girls at the party want to talk to you—"

The girls all had their hands over their mouths, trying not to laugh out loud, but Melanie hiccupped and the whole bunch burst out in one big giggle.

Steve moaned. "Oh, Stacey, I've got to get up at 6:00 tomorrow. You woke me up. Tell your friends to try someone their own age."

"But Steve," Stacey cut in, but the phone was already dead.

"Well, what did he say?" Jennifer asked breathlessly.

"He said to pick on someone your own age," Stacey said firmly, hanging the phone back in the cradle.

The group got suddenly quiet.

"Well, call him back and tell him Jennifer wants to talk to him," someone suggested.

Jennifer's pout turned into a sly little smile. "Yeah, Stacey! Tell him I'm your best friend. He'll know who I am. Come on, Stacey. Just one more call?" Jennifer smiled her do-it-just-for-me smile.

Stacey shook her head. "Why don't you call him, Jennifer? Girls call him all the time."

Jennifer wasn't impressed.

"Look, Stacey. Why do you think you're here, anyway? Steve's your brother, right? He won't mind if you introduce him to a few of your friends," Jennifer demanded.

Stacey felt like someone had punched her in the stomach. So Steve was the reason she had been invited. She should have guessed!

Stacey picked up the phone and slowly dialed the number.

"Hello, Steve? Stacey. No, I'm not calling for anyone else. I just need you to come and get me. Yeah, right now. Thanks." Stacey handed the receiver to Jennifer. "Come on, Julie. Let's get out of here," Stacey said finding her coat in the pile on the floor.

"But Stacey, what about the party?" Julie whispered loudly, trying to find her stuff and catch up to her friend. But Stacey was already up the steps heading for the front door.

"Jennifer's worse than a liar," Stacey shouted when they had gotten outside. "She's a fake! She only pretended to be my friend!"

Julie didn't know what to say as the tears streamed down Stacey's cheeks faster than she could wipe them off.

Stacey's prayer: I think I've learned a good lesson, Lord. Jennifer's not the only one who was a fake. I only wanted to be her friend because she's popular. I feel so embarrassed. Thanks for listening, Lord. I feel better now that I've told you. Amen.

4

Stacey hadn't wanted to go back to school on Monday but her parents insisted.

"Just be yourself," Mr. Simons said as he gave her a hug and dropped her off by the main entrance to the school.

Stacey was relieved to see Julie waiting by their usual spot. So was Jennifer and her tagalongs. They managed to mostly ignore Stacey and Julie as they walked past.

"You know, it's good to be back to normal," Stacey said, chuckling.

"Yeah, unnoticed and unpopular!" Julie joined in.

"You know, I used to think Jennifer was perfect, but now—well, I just kind of feel sorry for her," Stacey said seriously. "There's nothing worse than friends who like you only because it will make them popular."

"Well, you don't have to worry about that from me!" said Julie. "You couldn't have been more unpopular than you were at Jennifer's party! And I still like you."

"That's just what I mean, Julie. We're friends just because we like each other. I'm not sure Jennifer really knows what a friend is," Stacey said sadly, surprised at her own words.

Stacey managed to make it through homeroom, English, and even math, where Jennifer sat two rows over from her. Stacey watched Jennifer's black hair swoosh across the top of the desk in back of her.

Stacey didn't even bother to tug on her own hair. Somehow, swooshing didn't seem very important today.

The bell for lunch rang and Stacey joined Julie at their usual table. The two friends watched as Jennifer and her crew swooped down on another girl who just happened to have a 6'3" brother in high school who lifted weights.

"Think we should warn her?" Julie asked, watching the scene.

"Think she would listen?" Stacey asked, already knowing the answer.

"Hey Stacey and Julie! Any room for us?" two girls from homeroom yelled across the noisy cafeteria.

Julie motioned for the girls to join them. Stacey moved over to make more room. Two other girls from band filled in the other side.

Stacey looked around the table filled with trays, backpacks, cartons of milk, and smiling faces.

"You know, Julie, Jennifer may have it all, but I've got the best!"

"The best what?" Julie asked, moving her tray to the floor to make space for one more person.

"Friends," Stacey smiled brightly. "The best friends."

Across the room Jennifer Owens watched the crowded table as they laughed at one of Julie's jokes. For a moment a puzzled look crossed her face, but then she flicked her black hair over her shoulder and turned back to the girl with the brother in high school who lifted weights.

Stacey's prayer: Thank you, Lord, for friends who like me just as I am—warts and all. And Lord, help Jennifer to know you love her, too. Amen.

Action idea: Is there someone in your school or church that you think is "above" you, someone that you think would never want to be your friend? Something as simple as saying hi might be the start of a friendship you never thought you could have.

"Never ask, 'Oh, why were things
so much better in the old days?'
It's not an intelligent question."
—Ecclesiastes 7:10

•

*"Face it, Kim! You're just afraid to grow up!"
sneered Kelly. "Well I'm not and from now on
I'll do exactly what I want—with or without you."*

Something's Changed

1

"I'm sorry, Mrs. Adams, Kelly's not here," Kim spoke softly into the phone. "She said she had too much homework and was going straight home."

Kim paused as Kelly's mom asked more questions.

"No, I don't know where she is," Kim answered. "Yes, I'll call if she comes over later."

Kim hung up the phone and stood quietly by the hall table.

"Who was it, honey?" her mother asked from the kitchen.

"Uh—Mrs. Adams," Kim said in a halting voice. "She's looking for Kelly, I guess."

Kim's mother came out of the kitchen drying her hands on her apron. "You mean she doesn't know where she is?" Mrs. Carlson looked alarmed.

39

Kim shook her head. "I don't really get it. Kelly told her mom she was coming here after school, but Kelly told me she was going straight home today. I hope she's OK," she said in a worried voice.

"H-m-m-m. Sounds like Kelly's cooked up quite a story here," Mrs. Carlson said with a frown. "I'm not sure I approve of Kelly, Kim. She's changed a lot since last summer. I would really like to see you spend more time with some of your other friends, like Terri and Sarah."

"But Kelly's my best friend, mother," Kim argued.

"Are you sure, Kim? Sometimes friendships can change," Mrs. Carlson said kindly.

"You can't choose my friends for me. I'm old enough to know who's a friend and who isn't," Kim objected.

"That's enough, Kim," her mother warned.

"But mother—" Kim continued.

"We'll talk more about it at dinner," Mrs. Carlson said, returning to the kitchen.

Kim turned on the TV and tried to forget about the whole business of Kelly and the phone call.

But deep in her heart she knew that her mother was right. Things had already changed between Kelly and herself. Things they used to do together Kelly thought were boring now. Kim knew that Kelly's grades were slipping, too. Last week Mr. Jenner had kicked her out of class for smarting off. Kelly seemed to be proud of the fact and went around telling everyone what a nerd Mr. Jenner was. Kim noticed that sometimes Kelly's clothes smelled like cigarette smoke, too.

Kim climbed the steps to her room. Tomorrow she would have a good talk with Kelly. They had always been able to talk things out before.

Kelly hasn't really changed, Kim thought, trying to convince herself that what she already knew wasn't really true.

Kim's prayer: *Dear Lord, I guess if I'm really honest with myself, Kelly really has changed—a lot! I don't think everything she does is right, but that doesn't change the fact that we're friends. When does a friend stop being a friend? Amen.*

2

Kim hurried as she dressed for gym class. If she got done fast enough, there would be a few minutes to talk with Kelly before Miss Zimmer told the class to run laps. Kim scanned the old auditorium. A familiar figure slumped against the wall on the far side.

"Hey, Kelly!" Kim started in, "where were you yesterday? Your mom called my house and—"

"Yeah, I know," Kelly cut in. "She's already yelled at me about it, thanks to you." Kelly threw an angry glance up at Kim.

"Thanks to me? What did I do?" Kim asked, looking more than a little shocked.

"It's what you didn't do," Kelly hissed. "If you were really my friend you would have covered up for me."

"You mean *lie?*" Kim said, whispering the last word.

"Don't tell me you've never lied before," Kelly continued. "Thanks to you I'm grounded for two weeks!"

The girls sat silently, watching the rest of the class start the warm-up exercises.

"OK, maybe we got our signals crossed," Kim finally said, just to clear the air. "But where were you anyway?"

Kelly paused. "Uh—I went to the library and—"

Two girls Kim didn't know interrupted the conversation by yelling loudly at Kelly as they charged into two other girls standing nearby.

"Hey, Kelly! How about going over to the shopping center again after school today. Maybe we can get some more 'bargains' like we did yesterday," one of the girls said, nudging the other.

A look Kim didn't understand passed between Kelly and the two girls. The conversation stopped and all eyes turned on Kim.

"Who's your friend?" the girl with purple eyeshadow blurted out.

An uncomfortable look crossed Kelly's face. "Uh—this is Kim. Kim Carlson. Just someone I used to be friends with," Kelly answered quickly.

"Yeah, right. Catch you later, Kelly." The two girls began to run their laps as Miss Zimmer's whistle cut through the noisy room.

"I thought you said you were at the library," Kim said after the girls had gone.

"Listen, Kim," Kelly began.

"No, you listen," Kim said, more hurt than angry. "If you want to lie to your mother, that's up to you. But why lie to me? I thought we still were friends."

Kelly turned her eyes away from Kim and pretended to watch the runners.

"What's gotten into you lately, anyway?" Kim continued. "In case you haven't noticed, none of our old friends thought it was too funny that Mr. Jenner kicked you out of class the other day. Your grades are terrible. You smell like a pack of cigarettes. And I can just about imagine what kind of 'bargains' you picked up yesterday."

"Lay off, Kim," Kelly shouted into Kim's face. "You're not my parents, so stop acting like them."

Kim stopped and took a deep breath. "Look, we can talk about this later—"

But Kelly wasn't ready to give up quite yet.

"Face it, Kim. You're just afraid to grow up," Kelly sneered, her face as red as her hair. "Well I'm not, and from now on I'm doing exactly what I want—with or without you!"

Miss Zimmer blew her whistle and motioned to Kim and Kelly. "Get with it, girls," she yelled.

"Yeah, Kim," Kelly echoed, joining the girl with the purple eyeshadow. "Get with it!"

Kim's prayer: O Lord, am I really such a baby? Acting tough doesn't make a person more grown-up. I'm not going to lie and I'm not going to steal. And it looks like I'm not going to have Kelly as a friend anymore unless I do. Jesus, did you ever have any of your friends turn on you? Amen.

3

Terri, Sarah, and Kim all sat crowded on the canopy bed in Terri's room.

"She's really getting to be a pain," Terri said, throwing a pillow down on the floor. "It's like she thinks she can do anything she wants to. Did you hear she lipped off to Mr. Jenner?"

"Yeah," Sarah added. "And then she acted like it was a really big joke or something."

"I know she's got cigarettes in her locker, too. I saw them on the top shelf," Terri said.

Kim sat quietly at the far end of the bed, listening to Terri and Sarah talk about Kelly.

"And what about those 'super cool' new friends of hers," Terri continued with a hoot. "None of them can be passing any classes. I'm sick of the way they think they can get by with anything."

Sarah jumped over the bowl of popcorn and turned up the TV.

"Did you hear that two girls were caught shoplifting over at the shopping center?" Sarah said over the noise of the TV.

"Yeah," Terri added, "And they're thinking of taking away off-schoolground privileges for the seventh graders because of all the shoplifting at the stores."

"It'll be their fault," Sarah said. "They're going to ruin it for all of us!"

Terri threw a stuffed animal at Sarah and missed. "Kelly's group will have all of us sitting in the lunchroom twiddling our thumbs," Terri complained.

"Who says it's Kelly's group?" Kim said in a small voice. "Kelly's still our friend, isn't she?"

Sarah and Terri moaned. "Come on, Kim, she's already turned on us. It was her decision, not ours." The girls nodded in agreement.

"So some of Kelly's new friends are—" Kim started.

"Creeps!" Terri finished.

"OK, creeps," Kim agreed, "but that doesn't automatically make Kelly one of them."

"For your own good, Kim, will you face the facts?" Terri demanded. " 'Miss Super Cool' doesn't deserve your loyalty. When's the last time she's said anything friendly to you?"

Sarah popped the top off of a Pepsi. "Did she really tell her mother that she was going to your house and then skipped out?"

Terri and Sarah both looked at Kim, waiting for her answer.

"Well, yeah, but—" Kim started to explain.

"See, Kim! She's just using you for a cover-up, not a friend," Terri said seriously.

"I don't know," Kim said. "I still don't think we should turn our backs on her. Did anyone invite her here tonight?" Kim asked accusingly.

"Are you crazy?" Sarah laughed. "Do you want us to get a bad reputation too?"

"Watch out, Kim," Terri warned. "Hang around with Kelly's kind of people and others will start to think you're one of them."

Kim knew she was being stubborn, but she kept on. "Look, we don't even know if it was Kelly's friends who did the shoplifting. It could have been anybody," Kim suggested.

"Not me," Terri said firmly.

"Not me, either," Sarah said.

"What about you, Kim?" Terri prodded. "You're Kelly's best friend. At least you were. Would you tell on Kelly if you saw her shoplifting something?"

"Well, no. I mean yes. I guess I don't know," Kim stuttered. "I'm not willing to dump Kelly just because she's made a few dumb choices."

"A few!" Sarah groaned again.

"All right, girls," Terri's dad yelled up the steps. "Party's over. Lights out!"

Kim pulled her sleeping bag over into the corner of the bedroom. Kim pretended to be sleeping, but she could hear the other girls giggling and exchanging whispers in the darkened room.

"Kelly lied to me," Kim thought as she tried to get to sleep. "And now my other friends don't know where I stand. Who are my real friends?"

Kim's prayer: Lord, sometimes I feel like you're the only friend I have in the whole world. Amen.

4

Kim's stomach felt like one big knot as she walked toward school Monday morning. Ever since Friday night's party she had felt uneasy about facing Kelly and her new friends.

"Watch out, Kim." Terri's words played over and over in her mind. "Hang around with Kelly's kind of people and others will start to think you're one of them."

"But I'm not one of them," Kim said aloud to herself.

It didn't seem fair that choosing Kelly meant losing her old friends.

Why can't things be the way they used to be? Kim wondered as she took the shortcut through the alley behind the main section of the school.

Suddenly she heard voices. Kim paused on the first step of side stairwell and listened.

"S-h-h-h," Kim heard a voice whisper from under the steps. "Someone's coming!"

Kim leaned silently over the handrail, trying to catch a glimpse of the kids under the stairwell without being seen.

"Hey! Mind your own business!" a girl with purple eyeshadow yelled out from under the stairs.

Kim had seen enough to know that it was the same girls that had talked to Kelly in gym class. No doubt Kelly was hiding under the steps, too.

"Sorry," Kim said, pulling her head back from between the railing bars.

"It's your friend," someone whispered frantically. "Will she tell? Do something before she turns us all in!"

"Hey, Kim," Kelly said, stepping out from under the steps. "What are ya doing back here, skipping out?" Kelly laughed nervously as she dropped her cigarette on the ground and stepped on it with her heel. "Just forget you ever saw us, OK, Kim?" Kelly said, trying to look friendly. "Remember, we're friends, right?"

Kim just gave Kelly a sad little smile and began walking up the steps toward her first class.

"Are you going to tell?" Kelly called up to her. "Well, are you?" she repeated a little louder.

Kim opened the door at the top of the steps and walked through without looking back.

Kim's prayer: *Lord Jesus, It's hard to give up a friend. But I haven't really given her up—not for good. Maybe someday we can be friends again. In the meantime, Lord, please watch over Kelly. Keep her safe. I still care about her. Amen.*

Action idea: If you're having a problem with friends who are asking you to change—take a stand. Just say no. Practice saying no 10 times in front of your mirror every day. Then pray that God will give you the courage to follow through with your own decision.

"All your friends send greetings.
Greet all our friends personally."
—3 John 15b

•

*"That's it!" Kayla whispered excitedly.
"I'll refuse to make friends. Mom and dad will see
how miserable I am and we'll have to move back."*

Everybody Needs a Friend

1

Kayla Wright dug the toe of her tennis shoe into an anthill in a crack in the sidewalk in front of her new home at 212 Elm. The ants scurried in all directions as the sandy hill scattered left and right across the walkway.

"See how you like leaving your home!" Kayla snapped to the scurrying ants.

"Kayla!" a voice shouted from inside the house.

"Now what?" Kayla said to herself as she headed for the kitchen, letting the screen door slam behind her.

The late afternoon sun filled the cheery but cluttered kitchen still piled high with boxes marked "fragile" and "this end up." Carol Wright, Kayla's mother, was on her hands and knees, shoving odds and ends into the lower cabinets.

"Hi, honey!" she called without looking up. "How about unpacking some of the things in your

51

room before supper? You can't let these boxes stand there forever."

"I guess not," Kayla answered. She slowly climbed the long wooden staircase leading to the bedrooms upstairs.

It's not fair, she thought, slumping down against the side of her bed. *Why should I have to move just because of dad and mom?*

Kayla remembered the day her dad came home talking excitedly about a family-operated business for sale in a nearby town.

"Small bakery business—well-established in community—wishes to sell to interested party," her dad had read in an excited voice from that night's paper. "It's a good price, too, Carol!" Mr. Wright had said. "If we're going to move, now's the time—before Kayla and Kevin get much older."

"Older!" Kayla had interrupted. "I've only lived here all of my life. I've got friends, and what about my place on the gymnastics team next year?"

Kayla could still see the sad look that had passed between her parents.

"We know, honey," her mother had said, "but you'll make other friends."

Kayla pulled out the yearbook from her old school from the top of an unpacked box and flipped through the pages.

"I don't want new friends," she muttered, glancing at the familiar faces on the page. "If I can't have my old friends, I don't want any friends at all!"

Kayla sat quietly thinking about her old friends and town, then closed the book resting on her lap. Slowly a strange look came into her eyes.

"That's it!" she whispered excitedly. "I'll refuse to make friends. Mom and dad will see how miserable I am and we'll have to move back."

Kayla smiled a satisfied smile. Nobody would want to be friends with a grouch. And that's just what she planned to be—a grouch from now until their family moved back to where they really belonged. It was the perfect plan.

Kayla's prayer: Dear Jesus, I want to go home! Amen.

2

"Oh, knock it off, Kayla!" her twin brother Kevin said as they walked the three blocks to catch the bus for school. "You're acting like you don't have a friend in the world!"

"You've noticed?" Kayla said with sarcastic surprise.

"Yeah," Kevin continued, "and so has everybody else around the house. Maybe if you stopped scowling all the time and acting like such a—"

"A grouch?" Kayla said with a smirk.

"Yeah—a grouch!" Kevin replied. "What's with you anyway? You never acted like this back in—"

"Get used to it, Kevin," Kayla cut in. "I'm going to keep acting like this until we move back—toothbrushes and all!"

Kevin snorted. "Come on, Kayla. Dad and mom love it here. So do I. You would too if you'd just give it a try. There's no way we're moving back. You might as well face it!"

"We'll see," Kayla answered confidently, spotting the bus just ahead.

"You're doing it again," Kevin nagged.

"What?"

"Scowling."

"It's permanent," Kayla whipped back, narrowing her eyes into tiny slits.

"Have it your way," Kevin yelled back, running past her to catch the bus first. Suddenly, he stopped. "Hey, Kayla! Did mom tell you she was pregnant?"

Kayla's jaw dropped and she gave out a hoot. "You're kidding!" she yelled back.

"Yeah," Kevin laughed, "and you're smiling!"

Kayla clamped her jaw shut, her eyebrows moving even tighter together. Being a grouch wasn't going to be as easy as she thought.

Kayla's prayer: *Lord, it's hard to pray and be a grouch at the same time. Amen.*

3

"Hi, Kayla!" a friendly voice yelled from the back of the bus.

"Looks like you've got a friend whether you want one or not," Kevin whispered and then joined the guys on the boy's side of the bus.

There wasn't really a girl's side or a boy's side of the bus. It just always ended up that way—except, of course, for some of the older kids who sat with their girlfriends or boyfriends.

Kayla gave a half-hearted smile to Penny, who was still waving her hand trying to be seen over the mass of people who always got on at this stop. But Kayla pretended not to notice and sat down next to a rather round-faced girl with glasses who had her nose buried in a book.

She looks safe, Kayla thought, taking her science notes from her book bag.

A loud guffaw came from the other side of the bus. Kayla glanced back to see Kevin doubled over with laughter.

Must have been a good joke, Kayla mused. Back in Centerville, Kevin always told the best jokes. He and Skippy, Kayla's best friend, were always trying to see who could out-do the other.

Kayla glanced over at the round-faced girl still nose-deep in her paperback and then back at Kevin hunched over the back of his seat, trying to catch the next punchline.

"Oh, forget it," she said softly to herself, feeling more than a little left out.

56

"Huh?" the round-faced girl said looking up from her book with a puzzled expression.

"Oh—not you—I was—" Kayla stumbled over her words.

But the girl had already turned her attention back to her book, one of those awful teen romances that Skippy's older sister had always been reading. Back home, Skippy and Kayla had stayed up all night once reading out loud from *Love's Burning Embers*. Skippy could really be dramatic when she wanted to. It had been a riot. Especially when her sister came looking for her book!

"What are you reading?" Kayla asked, suddenly forgetting she was trying to be unfriendly.

The girl turned the book's cover just enough for Kayla's eyes to scan the dark purple script on the cover: *Love's Burning Embers*! It wasn't possible! The same book! Kayla managed to keep from laughing aloud only by faking a cough.

Unappreciated, the girl turned back to her page.

"Hey guys! What's green and red and all mixed up? Give up? A frog in a blender!"

The guy's side of the bus howled wildly while Penny and some of the other girls rolled their eyes back into their heads and groaned.

Kayla took a long breath, letting it out slowly. There was still an empty seat by Penny.

By the time Kayla had gathered her stuff and joined the other girls, Kevin was already half-way through his next joke. This time Kayla led the groans from the girls' side of the bus. Kevin turned to make a face at the group and spotted Kayla.

"You're smiling!" he mouthed, a look of mock surprise on his face.

"I know," Kayla returned, flashing him her full set of braces.

"Hey, Kayla!" Penny said, pulling a well-thumbed paperback from her pile of books. "Ever read *Love's Burning Embers*? I sneaked it out of my sister's room this morning. It's hysterical!

Kayla grabbed the book from Penny. "Try page 143—you'll die laughing," she said happily.

The round-faced girl turned and scowled as Kayla read loudly, "Darling . . . my darling . . . ."

It will never be the same as before, Kayla thought as she got off the bus and headed toward class with Penny and the others. But then again it might just be a whole lot better. It was worth a try.

Kayla's prayer: *Thanks, Lord, for helping me wise up. I'm glad that moving didn't mean leaving you behind, too. Now, Jesus, what can we do about the round-faced girl with glasses? I think she could use a friend, too!*

Action idea: It's good to have some time to yourself away from friends and other activities. But too much of anything is never good for you. Thank God for times alone and times with friends.

"There are four things that are too mysterious
for me to understand: an eagle
flying in the sky, a snake moving on a rock,
a ship finding its way over the sea,
and a man and a woman falling in love."
—Proverbs 30:18-19

•

*"Like David Thompson!" Megan said, her voice
rising a little higher. "Like David Thompson!"
she screamed convincingly. Dropping her voice
to a sudden whisper, Megan confessed,
"Actually, I think he likes me!"*

David and Megan

1

*I suppose Charles Edward has been in here snooping
again. Nothing is safe with Charles Edward on the
prowl.*

Megan threw the clothes off her bed and pulled
off her bedspread. Nothing. Lying flat on her stomach she groped under her bed for the book. Lots of
dust. One dirty sock. Two pair of tennis shoes.
Aha—success.

It had taken Megan two hours of dodging the library attendant on the west wing of the adult section
where the books on self-improvement were kept before she found it. *How to Make Yourself More At-*

tractive in Five Weeks: 172 Tips to Help Bring Out the Natural Beauty of Every Female.

Megan opened the cover of the oversized book.

Chapter 1: "The start of a beautiful woman is a positive attitude. Tell yourself you are beautiful and you will be!"

Megan groaned.

Right. Town tomboy. Tallest in my class. Why do they think I need this book if I already think I'm great-looking?

Megan began to have her doubts about Chapter 1.

"Megan MacGregor is beautiful," she said aloud.

Megan looked in the new full-length mirror she had gotten for Christmas.

Nothing. No change at all.

"Megan MacGregor is beautiful!" she said with more emphasis. The mirror hung silently from its shiny brass frame. Megan took a deep breath. This was not going to be easy.

"Megan MacGregor is—"

"Mom! Mom! Megan is telling herself she's beautiful. She's looking in the mirror, saying 'I'm beautiful, I'm beautiful'—to herself. Mom!"

It was Charlie. Ugly. Bratty. Eight-year-old Charles Edward MacGregor III. "My little brother," as Megan always introduced him to her friends. Megan knew she'd never seen an uglier face than Charlie's. She was sure he was adopted and her mom and dad just hadn't told her yet. His eyes were always pinched up like he had sand in them. And he was

61

constantly picking on a bloody scab on his chin. He usually needed to blow his nose, too. Megan looked. He did. Disgusting.

"Charles Edward MacGregor III, I hate you!" Megan screamed.

Not to be outdone, Charlie rolled his eyes upward and mimicked, "I'm beautiful, I'm beautiful," as he batted his eyelashes up and down.

That was it. Megan could take it no more. Picking up *How to Make Yourself More Attractive in Five Weeks,* she threw it at his scabby little face, but he was already halfway down the hall, chanting "Megan thinks she's beautiful!" at the top of his voice.

Megan's prayer: *Dear Lord, you've got to do something about Charles Edward before I do. Amen.*

2

"What a brat!" Megan stormed, summarizing her story about Charles Edward for Jodi.

"Disgusting," Jodi replied.

"Disgusting," Megan echoed.

Jodi and Megan were friends. They were also in the same homeroom—Mr. Kovash for language arts.

Megan glanced over at her friend. As usual, everything matched right down to the two yellow combs in her long, black hair. However she managed it, Jodi did not need any books on self-improvement. Megan sighed aloud and reminded herself to stop at the store and get some yellow combs after school.

The girls turned the corner and headed down Ellis Avenue toward Washington Elementary, or "Washington Middle School" as they called it now. There were too many kids at the junior high last year (or so the teachers said), and so the school board had voted to change the old elementary school across from Noonan Park into a middle school for grades 5-8. Most people still called it Washington Elementary, which made it very embarrassing when you had to explain to someone why you were going to an elementary school when you were in seventh grade.

"Really, Megan, I don't know how you take it." Jodi continued.

"What's that?" Megan replied, lost in her own thoughts.

"Charles Edward. Really, I don't know why your parents allow—"

"He's really not that bad," Megan cut in, feeling guilty about some of the things she had been saying. "After all, he's only little and he is my brother and—hey Jodi!" Megan blurted out. "Did you see who Mr. Kovash put me by yesterday? David Thompson! David Thompson—can you believe it?" Megan stuck out her tongue and tried to look as sick as possible.

"I thought you liked David Thompson," Jodi replied calmly.

"Like David Thompson!" Megan said, her voice rising a little higher. "*Like* David Thompson!" she screamed convincingly. Jodi wasn't impressed. Dropping her voice to a sudden whisper, Megan confessed, "Actually, I think he likes me!"

Jodi stopped and looked Megan squarely in the eye. "I've known it for a week," she said and continued walking.

"Jodi—if I think he likes me and you think he likes me then he probably likes me and—" Megan paused as the horror of that thought struck her. "Oh, no! He's going to know that I know! There's only one thing to do: act like I don't like him in case he thinks that I think he really does like me, or worse, that I like him!" Megan looked at Jodi to see if she had followed that rather confusing thought.

"Of course," Jodi replied matter-of-factly.

"Of course," Megan echoed, more confused than not.

"Well, here it is," Jodi announced. "Washington Elementary." Jodi rolled her eyes back into her head. "Disgusting. Really disgusting!"

Megan's prayer: Lord, sometimes my thoughts get so confused—even to me. I'm not sure what I'm feeling. Do you understand, Lord? Amen.

3

Clunk. Giggle-giggle.

They were at it again. Mike and Melanie passing notes inside their pens. It was an old trick, but one Mr. Kovash obviously wasn't aware of.

"How juvenile," thought Megan as she waited for Mr. Kovash to hand back her spelling test.

Clunk. Silence. Pssssst.

"Pick up the pen!" David's voice whispered from the desk across the aisle.

"What?" Megan whispered back in disbelief, but David's eyes were stuck on page 32 of *Captain Courageous*—the book Mr. Kovash had assigned for next hour.

Megan looked down on the floor. No doubt about it—it was his pen—an extra fine Bic retractable in a blue case.

"Nice work, Megan!" Mr. Kovash's voice boomed in her ear as she noticed the large "98%" on the top of her paper.

The unmistakeable sound of another pen being dropped made Megan jump in her desk.

Not now, David, she thought frantically. *Can't you see—*

Melanie giggled.

"All right you two!" Mr. Kovash's voice was stern. "You'll have to save your love letters for another time."

"Mr. Kovash," Megan began to explain—but he had already walked back to Mike's and Melanie's desks, picked up the pen, and returned with it to the front of the room.

"Pick up the pen!" a nervous voice whispered. It was David. "Open the note, there's a pen inside!"

Open the note? The pen—he meant the pen! Megan glanced to her right, but David's eyes were still glued to page 32 of his book. An unusual red color was working its way up his neck and into his face. The blue retractible still lay out in the open next to Megan's desk.

This is the pits! If I open his note I might as well stand up and scream, "I love David Thompson!" in front of the whole class. If I don't open it, David will think I really don't like him and that will be the end of it all anyway. If I had another reason to be down on the floor—Cautiously Megan pushed one of her books off her desk with her elbow. Thud! It was louder than Megan thought it would be. Mr. Kovash stopped and turned around to see what the commotion was. Megan smiled curtly and bent down to get the book and David's pen.

The note was wadded up inside the casing like a small pellet. It looked jammed, and Megan had no idea how to get it out. Taking the front of the pen and placing it in her mouth, Megan blew. Too hard! The small pellet shot across the room and hit Tim Wooten on the side of the head. He turned around and looked accusingly at Megan.

Please don't read it. Please don't read it! Megan prayed. Finding no one further to accuse, Tim turned back to his work. Megan hunted for the small wad of paper. Two paper clips, a broken piece of chalk, and David Thompson's note all lay together in the dust under Mr. Kovash's desk.

Megan's prayer: Boyfriends are sure different than girlfriends, Lord. Sometimes I think I liked David better before I liked him. Does that make sense? Amen.

4

Megan stood by her locker, trying to think of a way to get into Mr. Kovash's room and get David's note out from under his desk without anyone noticing.

Why do these things always happen to me? Mr. Kovash has probably found it by now anyway. I'll probably have to stay after school. It's not like I get notes every day. It could have been an emergency. I mean who's to say—

"Never knew my pen made such a great blowgun," David said.

Megan felt like she had just swallowed something too big for her throat. She couldn't breath, much less talk.

Think of something, dummy!

Megan managed a smile and went back to work on her lock.

"Here—what's your combination? These older lockers always stick," David said as he put his books down.

"32-21-33," Megan croaked out the numbers. *This can't be happening. David Thompson is opening my locker.*

Two girls from Megan's math class walked by and stared.

"Not bad—32-21-33," David chuckled.

Megan looked at him. *What did he mean, "Not bad"? My measurements? My measurements!*

"Ha ha ha!" Megan burst out too loud. The two girls who had passed by before turned around and whispered to each other. Megan took a deep breath. She definitely wasn't handling this well.

"Thanks for the help with the lock," she said, zipping up her book bag. "Sorry about your note. My brother Charlie calls me a windbag and I guess he may be right! Sure hope Mr. Kovash doesn't find it!"

"Aw—don't worry about it," David laughed. "All it said was 'Hi'!"

"You're kidding," said Megan, and then she laughed too. "And I was considering breaking in to get it!"

Megan looked at David. He was cute. That was a fact. Megan felt her stomach flip-flop twice.

"Mind if I walk part way with you?" David asked. His neck had that strange blotchy look again.

Megan stood frozen to the spot. Jodi and Megan usually walked home together, but Jodi had a piano lesson after school on Tuesdays so Megan was on her own. David looked uncomfortable as he waited for her answer.

"Sure. Why not!" Megan said, smiling. "I have to stop at the drugstore though."

"Right on my way," David said as they headed for the main entrance of the school.

Megan knew that David lived at 714 Kenwood Street and that the drugstore was at least two blocks out of his way, but she didn't think this was the time to get picky.

David and Megan crossed Urberg Street and cut through the old parking lot in back of the library.

"Charlie's your little brother, right?" David asked.

"Yeah—how did you know?" Megan answered with surprise.

"My little brother is in his class at school and he talks about Charlie all the time. I guess they give their teacher a pretty hard time sometimes." David winked at Megan knowingly.

They traded little brother stories, a couple of dumb jokes, and some mostly negative comments about school and managed to get to the drugstore without running out of things to say.

Megan looked at their reflection in the window of the drugstore. No doubt about it. There they were, reflected in the glass along with the toothpaste, foot pads, and Mike and Melanie. Megan blinked twice. Mike and Melanie were still there, staring back at them from inside the store. David saw them too, because his neck was all blotchy again. Tomorrow it would be all over school that David and Megan were a "thing"! Melanie was giggling and waving from inside the store.

Forget the yellow combs, Megan thought. "Just remembered—I have to sit with Charles Edward. Gotta run," she shouted back to David over her shoulder.

David shouted something too, but a car honked just then and Megan couldn't hear him.

David Daniel Thompson, Megan thought as she ran toward her house. *I like him. I like him a lot!*

Megan's prayer: *Lord, you created love so it can't be all bad! Thanks. Amen.*

5

"Any chips left from last night?" Megan asked as she rummaged through the cabinets in the kitchen.

"No. Charlie ate them when he got home from school," her mom replied.

"Figures," Megan muttered. Her parents didn't like it when she made negative comments about Charles Edward so she had to keep most of them under her breath. "Who's the little red-haired kid outside with Charles Edward?"

"Perry Thompson," her mom said, handing Megan a plate of cookies and a glass of milk. "He lives on Kenwood Street. This is the first time he's been over, although Charlie sure talks a lot about him!"

Perry Thompson? Perry Thompson who lives on Kenwood Street? Perry Thompson, David's little brother? Megan thought.

It was time for a closer look. But Megan was too late. Charlie and Perry had already come back into the kitchen looking for more to eat. Megan looked down at a red-faced little kid who was wiping his nose with his sleeve. He reminded her of Charles Edward and she handed him a Kleenex. Disgusting.

Ignoring the Kleenex, Perry asked, "Are you Megan that goes to Washington School and has Mr. Kovash for a teacher? Because if you are, my brother likes you."

Megan looked down at the squawky-voiced kid who had stopped wiping his nose only because he was too busy picking it with his finger. This couldn't be David's brother. Yuck!

"He likes you! He likes you! Megan's got a boy-friend!" Charles Edward shouted as he danced around Megan pointing his sticky fingers in her face.

"Charles Edward, you're disgusting," Megan bel-lowed, diving in his direction. Both Charles Edward and Megan ended up on the kitchen floor in one scrambly heap. Being more than a few inches taller, Megan had the definite advantage until Perry jumped on her back.

"Let go of Charlie. Let go of Charlie!" Perry yelled.

This little kid can't be serious, Megan thought. But there she was—down on all fours with David Thompson's little brother hanging on her back while Charles Edward chanted over and over, "Megan's got a boyfriend! Megan's got a boyfriend!"

"OK, you guys, that's enough!" Megan's mom cut in. "Megan, you're—"

"It's always me!" Megan shouted. "Charles Ed-ward started it. You heard him." Megan's eyes filled with tears. Perry was bound to tell David. Who would like someone that beat up on her little brother and then cried?

"Megan!" her mom called out. But Megan was halfway up the stairs, heading for the privacy of her own room. The mirror trembled in its brass frame as she slammed her bedroom door. Megan looked at her reflection in the mirror. Her face was blotchy. Her hair stuck out all over, and she had ripped the shoulder of her new shirt, too.

David and Megan

"Megan MacGregor is a mess—a big, fat mess," Megan shouted as she buried her face into her pillow and pretended not to hear the knock at her door.

Megan's prayer: *Isn't there anyone who really understands me, Lord? Amen.*

6

"Megan?" her mom asked as she opened the door a crack. "Can I come in, honey?"

Megan sat up on the bed but kept her face covered with her pillow. "Mom, I'm so embarrassed. I wish I could die!"

"It's OK, Megan. Perry's gone home and Charlie wants to say he's sorry," she said, stroking Megan's tangled hair.

"He's just ruined my life and he wants to say he's sorry!" Megan looked at her mother in despair. "I bet dad made him!"

"Charlie's still a little boy, Megan. And you—well, you're growing up. There's bound to be a few difficult moments between you two for a little while," she said.

"Perry's for sure going to go home and tell all about Charlie's crybaby sister who beats up on little kids," Megan said. Her voice came out in little gasps.

"Who's so important at Perry's house?" Megan's mom asked, smiling.

Megan paused. "David Thompson—Perry's older brother. He's in my class." Megan wiped her face with the back of her hand. "Mom? How do you know if a boy really likes you? I mean, I think he does, but how are you really sure? It's different from just having a friend who's a boy. And yet he's not a boyfriend either. At least I don't think so."

Megan's mom gave her a funny smile and said, "Well, if David Thompson really does like you, it won't matter one bit what his little brother goes home and says. He already knows you're a special person. And if you make a few mistakes once in a while, that's not going to change how he thinks about you. David's probably just as embarrassed about Perry as you are about Charles."

Megan's mom pulled her over and gave her a hug. "Why don't you wash your face and come downstairs for supper?"

"I love you, mom." Megan said with a shaky smile.

"I love you too, honey. You're a special girl and it sounds like David Thompson thinks so too!"

Megan could hear the phone ringing downstairs.

"It's for Megan, and it's a boy!" Charles Edward's voice rang out. "Hey Megan! It's a boy!"

Megan looked up at her mother. "What do I do?" she asked frantically. "It's probably David!"

"Answer it, honey," her mother laughed. "Just answer it!"

Megan's prayer: *I'm growing up, Lord. Grow with me. Amen.*

Action idea: Ask your mother, grandmother, or a special adult friend to tell you about her first boyfriend.

"All this is done by God, who through Christ changed us from enemies into his friends and gave us the task of making others his friends also."
—2 Corinthians 5:18

•

"There's nothing wrong with Kathy." Beth said. "She just tries too hard. It's embarrassing. You can't force someone to be your friend."

Stuck Like Glue

1

"Beth! Wait up!" a now-familiar voice rang across the crowded cafeteria.

Beth Bauer grabbed a tuna fish sandwich and a carton of milk from the cafeteria's food line and hurried over to the table nearest the water fountain. Stephie, Cheryl, and Mimi were already there devouring their lunches.

"Beth! Hey Beth!"

Plunking her tray on the table, Beth pretended not to hear.

"Kathy's calling for you," Mimi laughed as she jabbed Cheryl with her elbow. Both girls eyed Beth to see what she would say.

"Oh, just ignore them," Stephie whispered. "And ignore Kathy, too. Maybe she'll get the hint."

"Fat chance!" Beth said. "She's been dogging me everywhere. All I did was let her copy my English notes from last Thursday. You'd think I saved her life or something."

Stephie crunched on a carrot stick and nodded sympathetically.

"There's nothing wrong with Kathy," Beth continued. "She just tries too hard. It's embarrassing. You can't force someone to be your friend."

Stephie took a look over her shoulder. "Well, better think of something, 'cause here she comes."

"Hi!" Kathy said, sliding in next to Beth. Beth moved over a few inches. "Didn't you hear me calling you? Pretty noisy in here, I guess. Back in my old school you couldn't even hear the person next to you. It was a real zoo!"

Kathy looked around the table. "Oh, I'm sorry. I suppose you were all talking about something else and I just butted my way right in. Back in my old school my friends used to tell me I had 'foot-in-mouth' disease. It's incurable, but not fatal," Kathy said with a smile.

"How cute," Mimi whispered loud enough for Kathy to hear and continued stuffing potato chips into her mouth.

No one said anything.

"Uh—Beth, didn't you have to go ask Mrs. Chu about that physical science assignment?" Sarah suggested, giving her friend a sharp kick under the table.

"No, I already—" Sarah kicked her again. "Oh, yeah. Forgot all about it. Sorry, Kathy, I've got to go before the next bell," Beth said as she gathered her books.

"I'll come with you!" Stephie said as Beth jumped up. "I've got to call home to let mom know I'm staying after for volleyball practice again."

"You know, I think I saw my name on the science lab board," Kathy cut in. "Something about missing last Thursday's quiz. Maybe I'd better go with you, too."

Mimi and Cheryl moaned aloud, but Kathy didn't seem to notice as she threw her unfinished lunch into the trash.

"Uh, sure, if you want to," Beth responded in a flat voice. "Come on, Stephie."

Kathy talked all the way to the science lab. Beth didn't even hear her. She kept seeing the three of them reflected in the glass of each door they passed. *Can't Kathy see that nobody likes her?* thought Beth. *Who does she think she is, pushing herself on people? She must have heard Mimi's rude comments in the lunchroom. Why was she being such a pest? Can't she take a hint?*

"You know, Kathy—" Beth began, but Kathy just kept talking.

"You know, you guys have really made the move to Chula Vista a lot easier than I thought it was going to be. I mean, I really didn't even want to come here," Kathy continued. "You know, leaving friends behind and stuff like that. I thought it would take at least a year before anyone would even talk to me. But well—thanks to you guys, it's working out OK."

The three girls stopped in front of the science lab door. "See you later, Stephie. Coming Beth?" Kathy pushed.

"In a minute," Beth said. "I've got to talk to Stephie first."

"Oh, sure." Kathy looked slightly puzzled. "See you in class then, OK?"

"It's hopeless!" Beth whispered to Stephie after Kathy had finally left. "What are we going to do?"

"Beats me," Stephie shrugged. "She's your friend."

Beth's mouth fell open.

"Just kidding! Just kidding!" Stephie laughed. "I'll think about it and call you tonight."

"Beth! Hey Beth!" Kathy called from the other room.

Beth groaned. "Here we go again!"

Beth's prayer: *Dear Jesus, you had lots of people following after you, wanting to be your friend. Didn't you ever want to tell them to leave you alone? But you didn't, Jesus. Help me to do the same. Amen.*

2

Beth jiggled the lock to her school locker. Jammed as usual. *Not now, Lord!* she prayed. *I'm late already. I don't have my assignment done. Please give me a hand!*

"Can I give you a hand?" a cheery voice asked. It was Kathy.

Lord, aren't you listening? Beth pleaded silently.

"Back home at my old school my locker jammed all the time. It just takes sticky fingers," Kathy said, cracking a few knuckles. "What's your combination?"

Beth glanced up at Kathy and back to her lock. "Thanks, but I can do it myself."

"Oh come on!" Kathy persisted. "Let me try. I'm really good at it. Really!"

"OK! OK!" Beth said impatiently as she looked at her watch. Miss Lopez, the school paper adviser, wasn't very understanding when it came to being late.

"27-4-36. Got it?"

"Got it!" Kathy grinned as she gave the jammed lock a final jerk. "There, I told you I was good at it."

"Thanks!" Beth said with surprise in her voice. "I owe you one. Hey, look, I'm really late. Miss Lopez is meeting with all the page editors and I don't have my assignment copied over and we—I have to go. But thanks. Really."

"Sure." Kathy smiled slightly. "Catch you later. Maybe after school?"

But Beth was already lost in the crowded hallway and didn't answer.

"Well, it's about time," Mimi said, looking at the clock. "We'd almost given up on you."

"Sorry," Beth responded in a slightly out-of-breath voice. "My locker jammed again."

"I thought you might have run into little miss 'foot-in-mouth'!" Mimi chuckled.

The other editors looked up from their articles. "Foot-in-mouth?" Amy, the senior editor, asked.

"Mimi's loving this," Beth whispered to the girl next to her. "She has everyone's attention."

"Beth has a new friend," Mimi continued. "Kathy Webb. She's real friendly, isn't she, Beth?" Mimi smirked.

"Oh, lay off, Mimi. Just once, why don't you try being nice? I'm sick of you always cutting people down," Beth responded, her face growing red.

"Well, exc-u-u-u-se me," Mimi drawled out. "Since when did you start sticking up for Kathy, anyway? I didn't realize that you two were best friends."

"I thought Stephie was your best friend," Lisa remarked. Lisa was the editor of the gossip page. Beth could see it now. "Are B.B. and K.W. really best friends? Only Stephie knows for sure . . . ."

Lisa began taking notes.

"Oh, forget it, Lisa, and don't put anything in your column about it either," Beth said. "Kathy's just new in school. We're not best friends. We're not even friends!" Beth paused. "Can we get on with our meeting, please?"

"I don't know," Amy said as she stopped writing and looked at the others. "Maybe Kathy could be one of the people we were talking about before. Someone new, with fresh ideas."

"What do you mean?" Mimi butted in. "We have a full staff and plenty of reporters. We don't need anyone else. Especially someone who doesn't really understand the school like we do."

"That's just the point," Amy said. "We need to get out of our old ruts, you know? Who's the top basketball player for the week? Who made solo-ensemble? Who's going with who? We need somebody fresh. Somebody new."

"Not Kathy!" Beth exclaimed.

"Well, maybe not," Amy continued. "But we could use her for an idea Miss Lopez had for our next issue."

"What's that?" Lisa asked.

"What if we were to interview some new students? You know, get their impressions of the school. What they like. What they don't like—that kind of thing."

"I like it!" Mimi chimed in. Everyone turned in disbelief. Mimi never liked anything. "There's this new guy in science class I could talk to. He's real cute!"

"Never mind, Mimi," Amy said. "Just get the interview. And Beth, you could talk to Kathy."

Beth shook her head. "I'd rather not. Why don't you take it?"

"Listen, Beth. I'm already covering two other stories," Amy said. "If you don't want to write it, I can always find someone who does!"

Beth looked down at her books. "Never mind. I'll take it. But I don't have to like it!"

Beth's prayer: *Lord, it's hard to be kind when I'm in a hurry. Help me to be patient and take time for people. Even Kathy. And by the way—thanks for helping me with my lock today. Amen.*

3

Kathy was waiting by Beth's locker again the next morning.

"Thought you might need some more help with your lock," she said eagerly.

Beth took a deep breath. Her assignment was to interview Beth before Friday. *Might as well get it over with,* she thought. "Uh—no thanks. I got it myself," Beth said. "But there is something you could do for me."

"Sure, Beth, just name it!" Kathy beamed, glad to be included.

"Listen, we can talk about it on the way to homeroom," Beth said. Someone in a hurry rushed by, knocking Beth from behind. "That is, if we survive the early morning rush."

The five-minute warning bell rang.

"Better hurry," Kathy said. "I'll grab my books and meet you by the stairwell."

"No! Better not," Beth yelled down the hall. "There's a group of—" But this time Kathy was lost in the crowd, and so was Beth's warning.

Beth could hear the rowdy laughter up ahead. The throng of students heading toward class moved slightly away from the stairwell as they jostled past. The space under the east stairwell had turned into a gathering place for some of the tougher kids in school. It was best just to ignore them if a person didn't want any trouble. Beth could see Kathy waiting on the steps, watching the crowd move by.

"Come on, Kathy," Beth said, moving past the group of toughies.

As Kathy and Beth joined the flow of students heading for homeroom, they heard a long, loud wolf whistle followed by a nasty comment and laughter from the boys under the stairwell.

"Jerks!" Beth said under her breath. "Just ignore them, Kathy." But Beth's words were too late. Kathy had already turned and gone back to the stairwell.

"Come on, Kathy," Beth yelled over the noise of the other students.

Kathy was glaring. "Didn't you hear what he said?" she yelled back to Beth.

"They're losers," Beth said, taking Kathy's arm and turning her back the other direction. "Just forget them."

But it was too late. The boys had heard Beth's last comment.

"Hey guys. These two chicks think we're losers. What are we going to do about that!" one boy snarled.

A boy with greasy hair bumped purposely into Kathy, making her spill some of her books on the hallway floor.

"Leave her alone," Beth yelled. "Kathy, let's go now!"

"Not until they apologize," Kathy stood firm, her jaw set tight. A small group of onlookers began to form around Kathy, Beth, and the boys. The boys laughed loudly. Someone swore again as Beth started to push Kathy past a few of the group. The greasy-haired kid grabbed Kathy's arm as she passed.

"You want an apology? Here's your apology," he snarled.

Kathy gasped. A big wad of spit slid down the cover of her math notebook and onto the floor. The boys howled with delight!

"You creep!" Kathy yelled, pushing the greasy-haired kid back into his group of friends.

"Hey Jeremy! Gonna let a girl push you around?" someone yelled from the fast-growing crowd.

Jeremy's face was bright red. In one quick movement he reached out and slapped the rest of Kathy's books to the floor.

"Pick them up," Kathy yelled. "Pick them up or else!"

Jeremy just stood there grinning. "What are you gonna do about it, little girl?" he snarled.

"Pick them up!" a stern voice ordered. It was Principal Schmidt. "I've had it with you guys pushing people around here. Pick up their books, Jeremy, and then I'll meet you in my office." Turning to the group of students that had gathered to watch, he said, "Show's over. Now move it!"

"That was close," Beth whispered to Kathy.

Kathy looked anxiously through the things Jeremy had collected. "Where's my math notebook!" she asked in a frantic voice.

"I see it," Beth said eyeing the green notebook under the stairwell. "I'll get it for you. Must have been kicked over here in the shuffle," she said, kneeling down to pick it up.

"Isn't that cute," a sarcastic voice said. Beth looked at the pair of brown penny loafers that had stopped in front of her. "Look how they help one another. Just like best friends, right Cheryl?" Both girls giggled.

Beth looked around at the small group of kids remaining. Mimi, Cheryl, and Stephie all stood there watching. Beth began picking up the notebook, but her hand hit something wet. It was the gob of spit. That was it. Beth dropped the notebook back on the dusty floor.

"Pick it up yourself, Kathy! You got yourself into this. Not me. Come on, you guys!" Beth announced to the other girls. "We'll be late for class!"

"But Beth," Kathy's voice echoed down the nearly empty hall. The girls just kept on walking.

Beth's prayer: Dear Jesus, I blew it today. You wouldn't have been very proud of me. I'm sorry. Amen.

4

Mr. Richards scanned his homeroom class. "Anyone know anything about Kathy Webb?" No one even looked up from their books.

It's like no one even knows she exists! Beth thought to herself. Beth couldn't shake the uneasy feeling she felt every time she thought of Kathy and the incident in the hall a few days ago. Kathy hadn't been back to school since then. Beth had a strange feeling that it was because of how she had acted that day.

She glanced over at Kathy's empty desk in the second row. *Maybe something's happened to her,* Beth pondered. *She could be in the hospital, or maybe she moved back to the old school she was always talking about.* But deep down Beth knew why Kathy wasn't in school. She opened her math book and tried not to think about Kathy, the boys in the hall, and her own unkind words.

"It's not your problem," Stephie reassured Beth during lunch. "Kathy had it coming."

"But Jeremy what's-his-name actually spit at her. I mean, how gross is that? I still can't believe she actually stood up to those guys," Beth said, shaking her head.

Stephie put her elbows on the table. "Look, Beth. Maybe you were a little hard on her, but you got what you wanted, right? She's not buggin' you anymore."

"I'm not sure what I wanted," Beth continued. "I'm not sure I would have been so mean if Mimi hadn't made such a big deal about Kathy and I being best friends. And in front of everyone. I'm not sure why I did what I did." Beth paused. "If Kathy's not back in school tomorrow, I'm going to call her," Beth stated firmly.

"Well, if I were you I'd leave her alone. If you call you'll just start the whole thing over again," Stephie said as she gobbled down the last of her sandwich and left.

Kathy's seat was still empty the next morning. Beth waited until her study hall before she got up enough nerve to dial the number the school secretary had given her.

"Webbs," a cheery voice answered.

"Uh—hi! Is Kathy there?" Beth swallowed. A sudden lump had pushed its way up into her throat.

There was a slight pause from the person on the other end of the line. "Kathy's not—feeling especially well. Are you a friend?"

"Well—kind of," Beth answered. "We're in the same homeroom."

The voice on the other end of the line got suddenly softer. "Maybe you could help me. I'm Kathy's mother. I don't want her to know I asked you this, but—something happened at school a few days ago. Kathy won't talk about it except to say she's not going back." Kathy's mom sounded concerned. "You're the only one who has called. Do you know anything about it?" Kathy's mom hesitated. "It's just that I'm so worried about her. Things were going so well. She had said she was even making friends."

The lump in Beth's throat suddenly got bigger. "Uh, maybe she'll talk to me," she said in a quiet voice. "I think I can help. Tell her Beth is calling."

Beth waited a long time before Kathy finally came to the phone.

"Hello." Kathy's voice did not have it usual cheeriness.

"Hi. It's Beth. I'm calling to say I'm sorry. I really mean it. I can't believe I was so rude to you—especially after Jeremy spit all over your notebook. No excuses, Kathy. I'm sorry, and I want you to come back to school." Beth held her breath and waited.

"Look, Beth," Kathy finally answered. "It's not really your fault. I know I was being a pest, and I don't blame you for telling me off. You have your friends, and well—I guess—" Kathy stopped. "Well, you won't have to worry. I won't bother you anymore."

"Listen," Beth suggested. "Maybe we could both, well, start over. No more 'clinging vine' from you and no more 'kick her when she's down' stuff from me. OK?"

Kathy sniffed and then chuckled. "Sounds good to me!"

"Friends?" Beth asked.

"Friends!" Kathy replied.

"Great! See you Monday," Beth said in a relieved voice. "And Kathy—I'm glad you're coming back."

Beth's prayer: *Thanks for helping me have the courage to call Kathy today, Lord. I feel a lot better and I have*

94

a new friend instead of an enemy. You're the greatest, God. Amen.

Action idea: Do something this week to make someone feel included. Try it! You'll be glad you did.

"A rope made of three cords is hard to break."
—Ecclesiastes 4:12b

•

"You can't be friends with both of us, Jackie,"
Renee stormed. "Make your choice!"

Friends Forever

1

Renee Adler unlocked the cover of her five-year diary and carefully wrote "June 18" in the upper right-hand corner of the blank page.

Dear Diary.

Renee paused, her pen resting on the page. It was hard to know where to begin. So much had changed in the last three months—ever since Kristi Nicholson moved to town.

Renee scowled, thinking about Kristi, the cute new girl who had started classes three months ago at Central Junior High. Until Kristi horned in, Renee's best friend had always been Jackie Tenucci. Now everything had changed.

Kristi's ruined everything! Worse yet, Jackie actually seems to like her! Can't she see that Kristi's just trying to push her way in where she doesn't belong? There's only room for the two of us in this friendship. If Kristi's in, then I'm out!

Jackie and Renee had been best friends forever. They had even written a friendship pact three years ago. Renee had hers in a box under her bed. The pact was written in a secret code that only she and Jackie knew.

Renee chuckled to herself, remembering the time she wrote a note to Jackie using their special code. Mr. Cruz, their teacher two years ago, was dead set against passing notes. One day after several intercepted notes he warned the class that the next note would be read aloud in front of the others.

"I'm sorry, Jackie," he had said, taking the folded paper from the top of her desk, "I'm afraid you are going to have to be our example today."

Jackie looked mortified, Renee remembered, until Mr. Cruz opened the note. His face turned an unusual shade of red as he mumbled something about "just a bunch of gibberish" and threw the note into the wastebasket.

Poor Mr. Cruz tried all year to break apart the two girls. He moved their desks, assigned them to separate work groups, and even tried to break their code. Nothing worked.

Friends forever! That's what our pact said. And we both signed it.

Renee threw herself across the covers of her unmade bed. Most Friday nights she would have been sleeping over at Jackie's house or Jackie would have been over at Renee's house. Just the two of them. That's the way it had always been. Now Jackie had asked Kristi to sleep over, too. Renee was glad she hadn't gone. She didn't want to encourage Kristi any more than necessary.

"It's not fair!" Renee said to Jackie when she heard Kristi was coming. "We signed a pact—friends forever," she reminded her friend.

"Friends forever didn't mean *only* friends," Jackie had argued. "Kristi's really nice and she likes you, too."

Renee turned onto her stomach, pulling the pillow under her chin.

Kristi is nice, but it's not the same as just Jackie and me. And as long as Kristi's around, it never will be!

Renee stared at the empty pages of her diary for a few seconds and then began to write.

Dear Diary: It all began when Kristi Nicholson moved to town.

Renee's prayer: *Stealing friends should be just as bad as stealing money or other stuff. Is it wrong for me to want to keep my friend to myself, Lord? Amen.*

2

"Renee! Open up, it's me! Jackie!" a friendly voice yelled from under the old maple in the front yard.

Renee sat up and looked at the clock on her bedside table. "8:52!" she groaned. *Doesn't Jackie know this is summer vacation?* Renee thought as she pulled on jeans and a shirt from the pile of clothes on the floor.

"Surprise!" Jackie yelled, holding out a plate of warm cinnamon rolls. "Mom just made 'em. Don't they smell great? Let's eat!"

Renee yawned and looked around the yard. "You sure are up early. What happened to Kristi? I thought she slept over last night."

"She went home," Jackie answered. Her mouth was already full of roll. "She went to the city with her folks." Jackie swallowed the last bite of her roll and reached for another. "So what do you want to do?" Jackie continued licking the frosting from her fingers.

Renee stretched her arms up over her head and slumped down on the front step. "Sleep," she answered glumly.

"Eat first. Sleep later," Jackie coaxed, pushing the plate of rolls closer to her friend.

"OK! OK! You got me. I'm awake," Renee laughed. "How about going over to Grandma Timm's? We haven't seen her for a while."

"Yeah—or we could go over to the new pool. Kristi said they open early on Saturdays," Jackie suggested.

"How would she know?" Renee said in a voice that sounded suddenly harsh. "Kristi just moved here and already she thinks she knows everything."

"Well, she does know a lot of things," Jackie answered, unaware of her friend's growing anger. "Did you know she's taken violin lessons since she was four! That's why she's in the city today. She takes lessons every Saturday from a real violinist."

"I'm really impressed," Renee remarked in a flat voice.

"She's really funny, too," Jackie continued. "I've got to tell you this great joke she told me last night. I mean I was rolling on the floor. See, there were these two penguins—"

Renee leaned back on the front step and inspected the small hole she had just found on the knee of her favorite pair of jeans.

"Look," Renee explained. "I thought Kristi was going to be gone and we could spend the day like we used to—just the two of us. Now all you can talk about is how great Kristi is!"

Renee was surprised at the bitterness in her voice.

"Oh, come on, Renee," Jackie said, trying to smile. "Kristi's really neat. You'd like her if you just gave her a chance."

Renee looked her friend squarely in the eye. "I don't like people who go back on their word," she said matter-of-factly.

"What do you mean?" Jackie asked. Her voice was missing some of its earlier enthusiasm. "I haven't done anything!"

" 'Friends forever!' That's what we wrote in the pact. And you signed it. We both signed it! I don't remember Kristi's name on the paper," Renee accused.

"So we'll add it," Jackie suggested, "but we'll have to teach her the code first."

Renee stood up fast. "Add her name and teach her the secret code," she said, echoing Jackie's words. "Well, what if I don't want to? Kristi's your friend, not mine. Go ahead. Be her friend. Just count me out!"

"Renee," Jackie said in a hurt voice.

But Renee slammed the door to her house, leaving her friend alone on the front step.

Renee's prayer: Do I have any friends anymore, Lord? Amen.

3

Renee rang the doorbell and knocked twice on Grandma Timm's front door. Grandma Timm wasn't really her grandma. Everyone just called her Grandma Timm. She was that kind of person.

Renee gave the doorbell a couple more pokes, waited, and then walked around to the backyard. As usual, Grandma Timm was outside working with her flowers. Grandma Timm loved flowers. Morning glories, petunias, daisies, and her special rose garden all sparkled in the midday sun.

"Hi Grandma!" Renee called across the yard.

Grandma Timm looked up, waved, and smiled. "Be with you in a minute," she answered. "Just got a little more weeding to do here. Make yourself at home," she called over her shoulder.

Renee ducked under some spider plants hanging from their baskets on the old wooden porch.

Grandma Timm sure has a green thumb, Renee thought as she waited in the old rocking chair set out in the corner.

It wasn't long before the older woman came, wiping her forehead with the back of her wrist as she pulled off her well-used gardening gloves.

"Renee!" Grandma Timm said, giving her a big hug. "I thought maybe you had gotten too big to come over for visits with Grandma these days. Not too early for something cold to drink, is it?" she asked, heading for the kitchen.

Renee shook her head in agreement, and soon two large glasses filled to the brim with frosty lemonade were escorted out of Grandma Timm's large kitchen onto the back porch table.

"Beautiful out today," Grandma said, looking out over her colorful backyard. "The flowers are just in their glory—and so am I!" she chuckled, plucking a few dried blossoms from a plant nearby.

"You're always happy," Renee remarked, crunching ice from her glass. "Don't you ever feel sad?"

"Oh sure," the woman answered quickly. "Everyone gets sad, but it usually doesn't last very long. I have my friends—and my flowers." She paused. "Speaking of friends—where's Jackie? You two usually come visiting together."

"You mean my ex-best friend," Renee cut in.

"H-m-m-m," Grandma Timm said, setting down her glass. "Sounds pretty serious."

"Well, it's just that Jackie and I have always been best friends. Now this new girl, Kristi, wants to butt in," Renee complained.

"So where does that leave you?" Grandma asked knowingly.

Renee's eyes suddenly filled with tears. She was afraid to answer the question, so she sat silently kicking the toe of her sneaker against the porch floor.

"You know, Renee," Grandma Timm said, "Back when I first started gardening, I only planted rose bushes. I had tons of roses climbing over trellises and up the side of my house. I never wanted to plant any other flower because I was afraid if I tried something else it might not grow. I knew I could always count on my roses." She paused to see if Renee was following her thoughts.

Renee looked up and blinked a couple times. "So why do you have so many different kinds of plants now?" she asked, starting to count the assortment of pots and baskets scattered around her feet.

Grandma laughed. "Well, it just kind of grew, I guess. One at a time. First a friend gave me a few tulip bulbs. Then another friend moved and gave me her whole collection of African Violets. You know, each flower and plant remind me of a special friend. I sometimes think of this as my friendship garden."

"You have this many friends?" Renee asked, shaking her head in disbelief.

"Well," Grandma Timm laughed again, "not all at once. Some have moved and some have died now. But each person who I've come to know as a friend has colored my life in special ways. Just like these flowers do."

"A garden of friends," Renee echoed. "That's a nice thought."

"And you know," the woman continued, "roses are still my favorite flower. But I look out on all this beauty and I'm really happy that other flowers have come into my garden—flowers like you," she said, giving Renee a quick wink.

Renee looked down at her lap again. "I don't have a lot of friends in my garden right now," she said sadly.

"Your friends are there," Grandma Timm said warmly. "Just sounds like you need to start planting. And here's a little something to help you begin!"

Grandma Timm handed Renee a clear glass jar with a small, pink African Violet inside.

"It's beautiful, Grandma," Renee said.

"Just like you, Renee," Grandma added. "Now, why don't you give me a hand out back with the watering!"

Renee's prayer: Dear Jesus, thank you for Grandma Timm and her special friendship garden. Someday I want to have as many friends in my garden as Grandma Timm has in hers. But right now I need help replanting the ones I had. Help me find a way to make up with Jackie and Kristi. Amen.

4

"That's right—two o'clock at my house," Renee repeated over the phone. "No—it's a surprise. Just be here, OK? See you, Jackie."

Renee pressed her finger down on the button to clear the line and began dialing again.

"Hello, Kristi? This is Renee. Jackie's coming over this afternoon at two, and I was wondering if you were free to—You are? Great! Yeah—that's right. Two houses over in back of Jackie's—yellow with brown shutters."

Renee hung up the phone and breathed a sigh of relief. "Well, at least they're coming," she said quietly to herself. "Let's hope the next part goes OK, too."

At 2:00 Jackie pounded on the front door. Renee could usually count on Jackie to be prompt.

"So what's up?" Jackie asked, still a little miffed from the argument from the day before.

"Just thought we'd do a little gardening," Renee smiled mischievously.

"Gardening?" Jackie said in surprised voice. "It's the middle of June. Kind of late to start planting now."

"It's never too late," Renee said, laughing to herself. "Here comes our first little flower," Renee announced, glancing out her bedroom window.

"You're acting a little weird, Renee. If this is some kind of joke on Kristi, I don't want any part of it!"

"Oh come on—just trust me," Renee reassured her friend. "I've just been doing some thinking. Let's go down and answer the door."

"OK! OK!" Jackie said when all three girls were back upstairs in Renee's room. "Now what's the big surprise?"

Renee was already halfway under her bed, her tan legs sticking out from under the ruffled bedspread.

"Got it!" she yelled in a muffled voice.

"Is it dead or alive?" Jackie joked.

Renee pulled herself back out from under the bed, a small wooden box in her hand. "The friendship pact!" she announced, blowing the dust off the cover as she lifted the lid.

"What's a friendship pact?" Kristi asked, quite astonished at the whole scene.

"Just something Jackie and I cooked up a few years back," Renee explained. "It's written in code, but it reads something like this." Renee cleared her throat. "We do hereby declare that we shall remain friends forever till death do us part."

"Wow, you guys even have your own code. Maybe you could teach it to me," Kristi said excitedly.

"Sure," Renee offered, "but first we have to finish the pact."

Jackie's mouth fell open in surprise, but she kept quiet as Renee continued.

"You see, Kristi, Jackie and I have been talking. You know we've been best friends for a long time—and well—we probably always will be—"

"Friends forever?" Kristi said, finishing the sentence.

"Yeah—that's what the pact is all about," Renee said, laying the paper flat on the floor. "There's just one thing missing."

"What's that?" Kristi asked, a bit confused.

"Your name," Renee stated. "What do you think? Want to sign the pact? There's always room for another friend, right, Jackie?"

Jackie laughed a funny little laugh. "You're weird, Renee," she said with a broad smile.

"For sure!" Kristi said. "That is, for sure I want to sign. That is, if you're sure?"

"We're sure!" Jackie and Renee said at the same time.

Jackie began looking around the room. "Anyone got a red pen?" she asked.

Renee pointed to her bedside table. "Right there next to the African Violet," she said happily. "Now about the code—"

Kristi moved in closer trying to follow Renee's fingers as she pointed to the pact.

"OK," Renee began. "You move two letters over to the right from the letter you really want."

"Only if it's a consonant," Jackie added. "You move two letters to the left if it's a vowel."

"Right!" Renee said. "It helps if you write the alphabet in a circle to use until you get the hang of it. Ready?"

"Ready!" Kristi said, taking the red pen from Jackie.

"Friends forever!" the three girls chanted as Kristi Nicholson carefully added her name to the friendship pact.

Renee's prayer: Dear Jesus, today I feel like I'm blooming. Thanks for putting friends in my garden, Lord. Amen.

Action idea: Make a friendship pact with your friends. Look up in a Bible concordance to find what the Bible has to say about friendship. While you are at it, why not make a friendship pact with Jesus, too!